WILD WEST

HEROES AND ROGUES

VOLUME 1

WYATT EARP

The Showdown in Tombstone

By
MARSHALL TRIMBLE

AMERICAN
TRAVELER PRESS

Printed in the United States of America
2012 Printing

ISBN13: 978-1-58581-036-9
ISBN10: 1-58581-036-3

American Traveler Press
5738 N. Central Ave.
Phoenix, AZ 85012, USA
info@AmericanTravelerPress.com
(800) 521-9221

Wild West Heroes and Rogues Series

Look for more to come!

About the Author

Marshall Trimble's roots are rich in American military and lawman history. His ancestors were officers in the Revolutionary Army, fought under Andy Jackson at the Battle of Horseshoe Bend and the Battle of New Orleans. His great-great-grandfather, Moffett Trimble, rode with Bean's Rangers out of Fort Gibson in the 1830s and was later a Texas Ranger under the legendary Sam Walker during the Mexican War. His great-grandfather, Sam Walker Trimble, served in a Texas cavalry regiment during the Civil War and later fought with John Ford's Texas Rangers in the Indian Wars, taking part in the Battle on the Frio, in 1866. He was later a peace officer, professional gambler and stockman in Texas.

Trimble had ancestors outside the law, too. The notorious Texas border gunman, Charlie Small, was a cousin to his great grandfather. Small was gunned down by a Texas Ranger at Langtry, Texas in 1893.

Trimble's paternal ethnic roots are Scottish-Irish; his ancestors settled in Virginia in the early 1720s. His branch of the family then moved to Arkansas, finally arriving in Texas in the 1830s. His father, Ira Walker Trimble, was a third generation native of San Antonio, Texas, raised in the border towns of Del Rio and Langtry, Texas, before moving to Arizona in 1917.

Marshall Trimble began his career as a folk singer in the 1960s. After Doubleday published his highly successful book, Arizona in 1977, he returned to the stage, this time as a storyteller, cowboy poet and singer. He is, today, one of the state's most sought-after speakers and performers. He's taught Arizona History at Scottsdale Community College for more than thirty years and helped create the Southwest Studies Program for Maricopa Community Colleges. He's been director of that program since 1977.

This multi-talented historian can deliver everything from a serious history lecture to forty-five minutes of stand-up comedy. He appears frequently on radio and television as a goodwill ambassador for the state, and has opened for such acts as Rex Allen, Waylon Jennings, and the Oak Ridge Boys. "Trimble's Tales" are heard daily on radio stations around the state. He hosts the weekly television show, "Arizona Backroads." The show received a regional Emmy in Art and Entertainment Series for 2006.

He answers questions about the Old West from readers all over the world in True West Magazine's column, "Ask the Marshall."

This native Arizonan is the author of nineteen books on Arizona and the West, including the award-winning Arizona: A Cavalcade of History."

In recent years, Trimble has been the recipient of many honors. In 1999, he was inducted into the Phoenix College Alumni Hall of Fame. In 2000, he was selected as one of Arizona's representatives in the Library of Congress' "Local Legacies." Two years later, in Washington D.C., he received the first "Copper Star Award" from the State Society of Arizona.

The following year, he received the Scottsdale Jaycees' "Distinguished Service Award." In 2004, the Daughters of the American Revolution honored him with their Medal of Honor for leadership and patriotism. That same year he was inducted into Scottsdale's Hall of Fame, and the Arizona Veterans Hall of Fame. In 2006, as host of the popular television show "Arizona Backroads," he received a Rocky Mountain Region Emmy.

Wyatt Earp

O n a cold, grey October afternoon in 1881, four
armed men strolled purposefully down Tombstone's
Fremont Street. There had been a light dusting of snow
that morning and there was a brisk chill in the air. All
four were well-dressed. Three of the men, brothers, bore
a striking family resemblance—tall, handsome men with
blond hair and drooping mustaches in the style of the
time. The fourth man was slightly built, shorter than the
others, with a sweeping mustache and ash blond hair.
In contrast to the other robust three, his face had an

emaciated, sallow appearance. He was wearing a long, grey overcoat. Concealed inside the top coat was a sawed-off shotgun.

Down the street, between Camillus Fly's Photo Gallery and the Harwood house, five men dressed in cowboy garb waited, talking quietly. The feud that had been brewing for several months between the two factions had been mostly talk but the time for talk had ended. At this point neither side was in a position to back down. The grim-faced men didn't know it at the time but they were heading for a rendezvous with destiny. The events that followed would be indelibly frozen in time and etched in blood in the chronicles of Western history. It went down in history as the "Gunfight at OK Corral" even though it wasn't fought at the corral. It took place on Lot 2 Block 17, between Fly's Photograph Gallery and Boarding House and the Harwood house on Fremont Street, near the OK Corral.

No one knows for certain who made the first move. Street fights are like that. All hell broke loose, and for about thirty frenzied seconds there was blurred movement as shots rang out and acrid, white smoke filled the air.

When the smoke cleared away, three men—Billy Clanton, Frank and Tom McLaury—lay dead on the ground. Morgan and Virgil were wounded and Doc had a slight crease. The instigator, Ike Clanton, ran away.

The question persists: did either side really want to fight at that particular place and time? Neither side seemed set on a fight. The Clantons and McLaurys had been telling anyone who'd listen they were going to shoot the Earps on sight, but it sounded more like bravado over hurt pride. Also, they might have been waiting for some members of the gang to arrive. Or, as they later demonstrated, they'd rather ambush their foes than take them on in a stand-up fight. Town marshal Virgil Earp, the man in charge of the other side, was carrying a cane, hardly a weapon to use in a gunfight. And, as the shooting commenced, he shouted, "Hold, I don't want that!"

But fate was dealing the cards and likely some movement on one side or another set the event in motion. Historians are still searching for "truth." Perhaps that's why the "Gunfight at the OK Corral" continues to hold our interest.

Historians and Old West buffs still debate and discuss the wherefores and the whys of the feud. Most historians agree the Earps came closer to representing law and order than the group who opposed them, an amoral band of rogues known as the "Cowboys." But, the Earps have their detractors. A few go so far as to claim they were really "bad guys" who schemed and stole under the guise of a peace officer's badge, bullying the unarmed Cowboys into a showdown at the OK Corral.

The main players in this legendary shootout were Virgil, Wyatt, and Morgan Earp, along with their friend, Doc Holliday, representing the law and order element of Tombstone. Ike and Billy Clanton and Tom and Frank McLaury were part of a loose-knit band of cattle rustlers known as the "Cowboys," operating in and around Cochise County. The fight originated with Ike Clanton's fear that the Earps would expose him as a snitch who fingered the robbers attempting to rob the Benson Stage on March 15, 1881. The holdup was botched but two men were murdered in the attempt. Other issues also stirred the pot. Cochise County Sheriff Johnny Behan and the Earps were not only on the opposite sides of the political fence; Behan was a Democrat and the Earps were Republicans. They disagreed on how law and order should be brought to Cochise County. Behan had also reneged on a political promise to appoint Wyatt under-sheriff of Cochise County. There was a love triangle, too. Both Wyatt and Behan were intimate with the same woman, Sadie Marcus. Furthermore, Behan was friendly with the Cowboys and might have attempted to disarm them before the fight began. He would later say that he tried but they refused to give up their guns. Out of fear or design, he didn't, but he told Deputy U.S. Marshal Virgil Earp that he had disarmed them.

There were many sub-plots to this drama and that is why it continues to be one of the most fascinating events in western history.

Wyatt Berry Stapp Earp, was born in Monmouth, Illinois, on March 19, 1848, the third of five boys born to Nicholas and Virginia Ann Earp. He was named for Wyatt Berry Stapp, his father's commanding officer during the Mexican War. The oldest son, James, would suffer serious wounds during the Civil War and although he traveled to the far reaches of the West with his brothers, he didn't participate in the gunplay. Virgil, the stalwart, was the leader, but Wyatt was the most influential in the brotherhood. Their father had instilled a strong sense of family loyalty in the boys. They were clannish and didn't make friends easily. None were hard drinkers. The Earp boys also inherited a strong sense of adventure and restlessness from their father. Wyatt also had a younger sister, Adelia, born in 1861 and an older half-brother, Newton, born in 1837.

The four youngest boys—Virgil, Wyatt, Morgan and Warren—would live by the code of the gun. Warren and Morgan would die by the gun. Virgil would be crippled permanently by gunshot wounds in an ambush. Although he stared death in the eye on several occasions, Wyatt was never so much as scratched by a bullet.

Wyatt Earp was a product of the West, unlike many of his contemporaries, Eastern dandies who "wested" seeking fame, adventure and fortune, then rushed back East to tell their story to some eager journalist or pulp writer. As a youngster, he crossed the wilderness to California with his family. Twice he helped fight off Indian attacks. As a teenager he drove freight wagons over a treacherous 400-mile road from the port at San Pedro to Prescott, Arizona. During the late 1860s, Wyatt, by now a strapping, rawhide-tough young man over six feet tall, was working as a teamster on railroad construction and, on occasion a boxer, something that would prove useful in his future line of work.

The lawless towns young Wyatt frequented during those turbulent times weren't for the faint-hearted. As Mark Twain said of one, "It was no place for a Presbyterian...so therefore I didn't remain one." Many of the tracklayers and hunters were products of the violence and hand-to-hand combat of the Civil War. They'd seen death and killing up close and personal. Many came west because they couldn't exist in a civilized society. Lowbrow saloons served a fiery, tangleleg whiskey that could make a man go crazy, if he weren't crazy already.

By 1870, the Earp family had returned from California and were living in Lamar, Missouri where Wyatt, now 22, married a young girl named Urilla Sutherland. He was elected town constable, beating his half-brother Newt by a small margin of votes. It was the only elected office he ever held. Urilla died less than a year after they were married either from typhoid or in childbirth, leaving Wyatt grief-stricken. He never said much about his days in Lamar and after her death spent the next couple of years drifting.

Like many of his ilk, Wyatt wasn't always on the side of the law. He became involved in a March 1871 incident that caused detractors to later claim he was a horse thief in eastern Oklahoma. If he did participate in the theft of a couple of horses, it was a youthful mistake. No federal warrant was ever issued for him. He was charged and skipped bail. New evidence indicates he escaped from jail and was never tried. This might have been a crossroads for him. He might have become an outlaw but chose to go the other way. Like a lot of restless youths who might have gone bad, he learned a good lesson from his mistake and took another trail.

Also, there is new evidence that Wyatt was arrested for pimping in Peoria, Illinois at the same time later myth-makers had him out west.

Wyatt was hunting buffalo down on the Arkansas River in early 1871 when he met Bat Masterson and his brother Ed. The men struck up a fast friendship and would later work as lawmen in Dodge City. Ed was later killed in the line of duty and Wyatt and Bat remained friends until Masterson died in 1921. Wyatt missed out on the buffalo hunt with Billy Dixon and Bat Masterson in 1874, thus missing the famous battle at Adobe Walls against Quanah Parker's Comanche warriors. This was the fight where Dixon made his famous long shot. Using a .50 caliber Sharps, Billy Dixon emptied a Comanche saddle from the unbelievable distance of 1,538 yards. Not surprising, it was the last shot of the fight as the warriors withdrew.

Next, Wyatt headed for Ellsworth, Kansas. By 1873, Ellsworth had replaced Abilene as the main trail's end town for the drovers from Texas to deliver their cattle. It was in Ellsworth where Wyatt later claimed to have had his famous confrontation with the notorious Ben Thompson. Some say the story is a fabrication while others say there is evidence to say it did, just not as dramatic as Wyatt's biographer, Stuart Lake, wrote it.

Trouble began on August 15 when Ben Thompson got into an altercation with some corrupt local lawmen over a game of cards. His brother Billy, staggering drunk, grabbed Ben's shot gun and joined the fight. Ben and Billy and the rest of the Texans drew their guns on the locals, creating a standoff. Unarmed, County Sheriff Chauncey Whitney tried to play the peacemaker but was accidentally shot and fatally wounded by a drunken Billy Thompson. "My God, Billy," Ben yelled, "you have shot our best friend."

Wyatt claimed that after Whitney went down, the Ellsworth mayor appointed him marshal and pinned a badge on him. This time Wyatt, played the peacemaker, and calmly convinced Ben that he should give it up. Ben agreed, paid a small fine and left town with a respect for the coolness of Wyatt. It was not a Hollywood-type showdown but it says a lot about Wyatt's steadiness under fire. The best and most respected lawmen were those who could diffuse a tense situation and not have to resort to gunplay.

In the aftermath, Billy hid from the law in Texas for three years before Texas Rangers arrested him and extradited him to Kansas for trial, where he was declared not guilty.

Wyatt's next stop was Wichita where, during the cattle shipping season of 1874, town Marshal Bill Smith hired him as a part-time officer. When Mike Meagher was elected marshal in 1875, Wyatt became a deputy; his service was exemplary. By now, Virgil, Morgan and Jim were all residents of the town. Jim's wife, Bessie, was running a bordello in Wichita.

Despite his good record, politics got him canned the following year when Smith ran again. During the campaign, he made some remarks about the Earp family and Wyatt went about settling the matter with his fists. Meagher fired him for disturbing the peace. After he won re-election, Meagher tried to re-appoint Wyatt, but the town council was deadlocked on the issue so the marshal continued to use him for part-time peace-keeping. By 1876, Wichita was on the wane as a cow town as the shipping points were moving west.

Testimony to Wyatt's service in Wichita was complimentary of his character. Dick Cogdell, the man who succeeded Meagher as marshal later said of Wyatt, "Earp is a man who never smiled or laughed. He was the most fearless man I ever saw… He is an honest man. All officers here who were associated with him declare that he is honest…"

Wichita Deputy Jimmy Cairns, who served with him added, "Wyatt Earp was a wonderful officer. He was game to the last ditch, and apparently afraid of nothing. The cowmen all respected him and seemed to recognize his superiority and authority at such times as he had to use it."

The next stop for Wyatt was Dodge City, the "Queen of the Cow Towns." Earp biographer Casey Tefertiller said of the town, "If Wichita was wicked, Dodge was Sodom itself, with no pretense of being anything else."

The town was infested with the worst dregs of frontier society and law enforcement was non-existent.

The heyday of the cattle business in Dodge City began in 1876. Although no records remain, newspaper accounts mention Wyatt as assistant marshal at various times over the next couple of seasons. He was joined by the Masterson brothers, Bat, Jim and Ed. Ed, acting as city marshal would be killed in the line of duty on April 8, 1878 by a drunken Texas cowhand.

In October 1877, Wyatt drifted through Indian Territory and into the Texas town of Fort Griffin where he first met Doc Holliday.

Doctor John Henry Holliday was a dentist by trade. He was born in 1852 in Griffin, Georgia, into a prosperous Southern family and had graduated from dental school in Philadelphia. Eventually, he opened a practice in Texas, but he'd contracted tuberculosis, something that limited his work and he began to spend more time at the card tables. At times Doc was a true Southern gentleman and at others a reckless drunk with an out-of-control temper. He was educated and had a good sense of humor but he was also hot-headed and impetuous. In short, Doc was a walking contradiction. He headed west in hopes the dry climate might prolong his life. Somewhere along the way he paired up with a prostitute named Mary Katherine Horony, better known as Big Nose Kate Elder.

Wyatt told a story about his first meeting with Holliday at Fort Griffin when Doc was playing cards with a man named Bailey. Doc caught Bailey cheating and told him to "play poker." In gambler's lingo, this was a polite way to say, "Quit cheating." Bailey didn't take heed and Doc pulled in the pot. Bailey went for his gun. Quick as a flash, Doc pulled a knife and made a deep slash in Bailey's brisket. The town marshal and his constables then confined Doc in the lobby of a local hotel while a band of angry citizens outside were planning a necktie party.

Doc Holliday

When Kate learned of Doc's predicament, she tied a couple of horses out back of the hotel and set fire to a nearby shed. Then she hollered "Fire!" When everybody's attention was diverted, Kate pulled a gun on the lawmen and rescued her lover.

It's a good story but it has no basis for truth. Kate herself denied it ever happened. One has to always keep in mind, storytelling and exaggeration was considered a cherished right by old-timers, including the famous and not-so-famous.

Wyatt and Doc began what would be a long friendship. Wyatt claimed later the bond was established when Doc backed his play and covered his backside one night in Dodge City. A couple of Texas cowhands named Driskill and Morrison were on the prod, threatening Wyatt. They cornered him just outside the Long Branch Saloon. Doc was playing cards inside when he heard the ruckus. He grabbed his six-shooter and pushed through the swinging doors, swearing an oath that would have caused a mule-skinner to blush. The cowboys were distracted long enough for Wyatt to lay his pistol barrel up beside Morrison's head. When one of the cowboy's friends took a pot shot at Wyatt, Doc plugged him in the shoulder.

"One thing I've always believed," Wyatt said. "If it hadn't been for Doc Holliday, I'd have cashed in that night."

The Earps, especially Wyatt and Morgan, were among the very few Doc could call friends. The irascible, cantankerous Holliday seems to have placed much value on this friendship.

Bat Masterson said, "His whole heart and soul were wrapped up in Wyatt Earp and he was always ready to stake his life in defense of any cause in which Wyatt was interested."

Wyatt's tolerance of Doc during his bouts with booze and violent outbursts was a credit to his patience. Also, Doc's association with some shady characters would prove to be a source of embarrassment to Wyatt in the years to come. Many of Wyatt's problems in Tombstone were the result of his friendship with Doc, or in the defense of Doc. Through it all, the two remained steadfast friends.

Following the killing of Ed Masterson in April 1878, assistant marshal Charlie Bassett became city marshal. He appointed Wyatt as his chief assistant. Wyatt's appointment received glowing accounts in the local press. The Ford County Globe wrote, "Wyatt Earp, one of the most efficient officers Dodge ever had, has just returned from Fort Worth, Texas. He was immediately appointed Assistant Marshal by our city dads, much to their credit."

The toughest part about enforcing the law in a town like Dodge was keeping the peace without discouraging business. This caused peace officers to have to walk a fine line. Bat Masterson, Wyatt and the others were more prone to wrapping their pistol barrels along the head of a troublemaker than firing their weapons. This was known as "Buffaloing." Dead cowboys couldn't spend money in the saloons, lose money at the gambling tables or keep the business of prostitution thriving.

But by 1879 Dodge was fading the way of its predecessors, Abilene, Ellsworth, and Wichita. The cattle business was declining, settlers were moving in, and temperance workers were trying to dry out the town. It was time for the restless ones to move on. Virgil had moved to Prescott, Arizona, and the rich silver boom town of Tombstone beckoned.

The raucous, bibulous Gomorrah of a silver camp on Goose Flat that folks were beginning to call Tombstone was just beginning to feel its oats in early 1880. The town, located on a mesa a few miles east of the San Pedro River, some 75 miles east of Tucson, was experiencing prosperity unsurpassed in the history of Arizona. The great silver strike was cause for talk of creating a new state with Tombstone as the capital. Some 2,000 would-be millionaires pitched tents, wickiups, shanties and set about the business of getting rich without working. Saloons and gambling halls on Allen Street were wide open for business 24 hours a day.

Tombstone became a gathering place for the wide gamut of frontier society that ranged from mining and real estate speculators, entrepreneurs of all kinds, merchants, preachers and teachers to prostitutes, cattle rustlers, con men, swindlers and tin horn gamblers.

Like many others, the Earp brothers came to Tombstone seeking their fortune. James, Virgil, Wyatt and Morgan arrived in December 1879, and began investing in mining claims, town lots and water rights. They were accompanied by their women, Bessie, Allie, Mattie and Louisa. Doc Holliday and Big Nose Kate remained in Prescott and didn't arrive in Tombstone until the following September.

Virgil Earp had been a peace officer in Prescott for a couple of years prior to moving to Tombstone and was persuaded by U.S. Marshal Crawley P. Dake to take a deputy marshal's position in Tombstone. During his first few months in Tombstone, Wyatt took a job riding shotgun for Wells Fargo. On July 27, 1880, Pima County Sheriff Charlie Shibell appointed Wyatt deputy for the Tombstone district. Tombstone was still a part of Pima County until the creation of Cochise County on February 1, 1881. There were some trials held in Tombstone but the more serious cases were tried at the county seat in Tucson. Still, Wyatt was an effective lawman. His efforts to keep the peace in the raucous mining camp were mentioned frequently in the local newspapers.

The southeast corner of Arizona that was to become Cochise County had also become a favorite stamping ground for desperadoes, driven to the remote region as civilization and the law moved west. The rugged terrain near the Mexican border was an ideal place to hide stolen cattle. Ranchers on both sides of the border were victimized by a large, loosely-organized pack of rustlers that operated under a number of leaders, including a hard-bitten rascal known as "Old Man" Clanton.

Newman Haynes Clanton and his sons, Ike, Billy and Fin, along with two brothers Tom and Frank McLaury, used their ranches as clearing houses for stolen cattle in the San Pedro and Sulphur Springs Valleys. They would purchase stolen livestock, re-brand and re-sell.

The "Cowboys," as they were known, numbered about fifty. Included among them was Johnny Ringo, one the greatest names among gunfighters.

Historians would be hard-pressed to find a gunfighter more glorified and less-deserving than Johnny Ringo. He is, arguably, the most over-rated gunfighter in the Old West. He's been called the "Classic cowboy-gunfighter," the "King of the Cowboys," and described as a "strictly honorable man whose word was his bond." "Fearless in the extreme," another wrote. This grade school drop-out has also been referred to as an avid reader of good books, and a noble "real life Don Quixote" who read Shakespeare. None of this is true. Ringo was described as a deadly, morose killer, yet his only proven killing was in the Texas Hoodoo War and that was a cowardly act. On September 25, 1875, he and a man named Williams rode up to James Cheyney's place. Cheyney was rumored to have set up a couple of their friends for murder. Cheyney was washing his face and while his face was covered with a towel they gunned him down in cold blood. They were later tried for murder but, as so often happened in range wars, the charges were dismissed. That seems to be the King's only gunfight. Of course, the Mason County War had several shootouts and Ringo may have participated in them. And he might have killed Mexicans during the raids into Sonora by the "Cowboys," but these were ambushes rather than gunfights.

Another cowboy whose reputation was overblown was William Brocius, better known as "Curly Bill." In reality, no one knows for certain what his real name was, as he used a number of aliases in his lifetime. His gregarious personality made him a Cochise County popular figure. Cochise County Deputy Sheriff Billy Breakenridge described him as being "fully six feet tall, with black curly hair, freckled face and well built." No documented photos have been found and there are no details regarding his mother and father. In short, he was a mysterious man from no place.

His origins are uncertain but as a young man he drifted into Texas where he worked as a cowhand, and then on to New Mexico where he derived his colorful nickname from a cantina girl who was enthralled by his dark, curly hair. Like Ringo, Curly Bill had an inflated reputation as a gunslinger. He was more of an outlaw than a man-killer. In fact, he may have only killed one man in his career, but the outlaws of Cochise County were a hard breed of men and the fact that Curly Bill was their leader says something of his toughness. He was also known as the "Outlaw King of Galeyville," a small mining town on the eastern side of the Chiricahua Mountains in Cochise County. Despite the popular notion, Galeyville wasn't an "outlaw town." Curly Bill and his friends weren't really a public nuisance. They were smart enough to avoid trouble most of the time and the local saloons were happy to have their business. Curly Bill got into an altercation there on May 25, 1881 with a cowboy from New Mexico named Jim Wallace. When Curly Bill stepped out of a saloon, Wallace bushwhacked him. The bullet struck Curly Bill in the cheek, went through and came out the other side of his mouth, taking some teeth. It looked for a while like the outlaw king was going to die and his friends made plans to string up Wallace. But Curly Bill had a strong constitution and he survived, although he did have to spend the next few weeks with an awkward bandage wrapped around his head. This injury could been the reason why he was nowhere near Tombstone on October 26, 1881.

Curly Bill figured prominently in the outlawry along the Mexican border in the early 1880s. He was personally responsible for rustling thousands of Mexican longhorns and earned the dubious distinction of having his name mentioned in a number of hotly-worded diplomatic notes exchanged between the U.S. and Mexico. Newspapers at the time hailed him as the "most famous outlaw in Arizona."

Stealing livestock wasn't the Cowboys only stock in trade. Mexican smugglers along the border were another prey as were stagecoaches rumbling along the lonely roads leading to and from Tombstone loaded with payroll or bullion from the mines.

After Mexico increased taxes on alcohol and tobacco in the late 1870s, smuggling became big business. Mexican smugglers exchanged silver and gold in Tucson and other trading posts for alcohol and tobacco to sell below border. The smugglers became easy prey for the "Cowboys." Also, huge profits were made by the Cowboys by their raiding into Mexico and rustling cattle.

Two Cowboys from Galeyville named "Mac" McAllister and George Turner got a contract to supply beef to Fort Bowie at the north end of the Chiricahua Mountains. Then, with a small band of cowboys, they headed for Mexico and stole some 500 head from rancher Juan Vasquez. Soon, Vasquez and his men caught up with the rustlers and killed them, but in the fight the rancher was gunned down. Emotions were running high on both sides of the border.

When the Mexicans clamped down on border crossings, the Cowboys turned their violence loose on the American side. Claiming it was a matter between the Cowboys and civil authorities, the American military refused to intervene. And grand juries couldn't bring charges because witnesses were afraid to testify.

The shooting of President James Garfield on July 2, 1881, and his lingering until death on September 19, paralyzed the government and, by the time his successor Chester Arthur took the reins of government, roving bands of renegade Apache were stirring up trouble so the serious problems with outlawry were kept on the back burner.

The rush of population to Tombstone had created a beef bonanza. The outlawry was widespread, the thieves so brazen that cattle were being pilfered in broad daylight.

Wyatt wasn't exempted from the thievery, either.

Young Billy Clanton greeted the former Kansas lawman soon after his arrival by stealing Wyatt's favorite horse, Dick Naylor.

In mid-July, 1880, six mules were stolen from the army at Fort Rucker, about seventy-five miles east of Tombstone in the Chiricahua Mountains. Lieutenant J. H. Hurst rode into Tombstone and asked U. S. Deputy Marshal Virgil Earp's assistance in recovering the animals. Virgil, Wyatt, and Morgan, with Wells Fargo agent Marshall Williams, along with the officer and four soldiers, tracked the mules to a ranch on Babocomari Creek, owned by Tom and Frank McLaury. They arrived to find the thieves altering the US brand to a D8. Hurst was told the mules would be returned if no arrest was made. There were fifteen or twenty rustlers holed up at the ranch, so to avoid bloodshed the officer accepted the deal but the mules were never returned. The McLaury brothers hadn't stolen the mules but were offering sanctuary to the thieves who had.

When the mules weren't returned, Lieutenant Hurst publicly accused and named the thieves, Pony Deal (sometimes spelled Diel), and two others. He also charged Frank McLaury with helping hide the animals. McLaury angrily responded to the charges by accusing the officer of stealing the mules. This pattern of responding to charges by reversing the charge was common practice by the outlaws and would be used to tarnish the Earps' reputations in the months to come.

Virgil, who'd been acting in his role as U.S. Deputy Marshal in connection with the theft, said that McLaury asked him later if he had had anything to do with Hurst's public accusation. When told "No," McLaury admitted that he planned to kill the marshal if he had.

Virgil Earp

Several months later, Wyatt, acting on a tip, learned his horse was in the nearby town of Charleston. Wyatt rode over and found his horse in a local corral. He wired his brother Jim to get the proper paperwork to recover the horse. Meanwhile, Billy Clanton learned Wyatt was in town and attempted to take the horse out of the corral. Wyatt stopped him, saying the papers were coming that would prove ownership. Billy brazenly asked if he had anymore horses to lose. Wyatt replied that in the future he'd keep his horse in a stable so the youngster would not be able to steal them.

The horse, Dick Naylor, would play a role in another incident on January 14, 1881. Virgil rode him out to check on some mining claims and, on the road to Charleston, encountered the town constable on the San Pedro in a buckboard with a young prisoner. The constable told Virgil that a lynch mob was on his tail. The prisoner, a tin horn gambler they called Johnny-Behind-the-Deuce (actually, Mike O'Rourke), had killed a local in self-defense, but the citizens of Charleston had taken umbrage at the action and were bent on hanging the youngster.

Virgil raced into Tombstone with the prisoner riding behind and gave him to Wyatt to protect from the mob. By most accounts, Wyatt grabbed a Wells Fargo shotgun and took the gambler to a local bowling alley while a mob from Charleston gathered outside. With several lawmen forming a circle around the prisoner, Wyatt, shotgun in hand led them through the mob, saying "Stand back there and make passage. I'm taking this man to jail in Tucson."

When the mob tried to halt them, Wyatt pointed his shotgun at one of the mining district's leading citizens, Richard Gird, and warned them that if they attacked the posse he would shoot Gird. The crowd backed off and Johnny-Behind-the-Deuce was taken to Tucson. It was the kind of standoff between lawman and mob that would be re-played many times in twentieth century movies and television shows.

Incidentally, Johnny-Behind-the-Deuce never stood trial. He escaped from jail and that was the last anybody heard from him.

Trouble erupted again on a late October evening in 1880 when Curly Bill and some of his friends were firing off their pistols in Tombstone, a violation of the town ordinance. Up to then, Brocius was a relatively unknown cow thief. What followed would make him one of Cochise County's most notorious figures.

City marshal Fred White ordered Curly Bill to surrender his pistol. When the outlaw pulled it from his holster, White grabbed the barrel and it went off, hitting him in the groin. Stories would later be told he offered the pistol butt forward but as White reached out, Curley Bill spun it around so the barrel was pointed at the marshal and when the officer grabbed the barrel, it went off. Supposedly that's where the so-called "Curly Bill Spin" was born.

At the first sound of gunfire, Wyatt borrowed a pistol from Fred Dodge and rushed to White's assistance, arriving just as the lawman was shot. Wyatt "buffaloed" or knocked Curly Bill to the ground with a blow to the head from Wyatt's pistol barrel.

Fearing a lynch mob Wyatt, Morgan and Dodge hustled Curly Bill off to jail. They guarded the jail closely that night to keep White's friends from getting any ideas. The next day, Wyatt escorted him to Tucson where he'd be safe from the mob. Marshal White, on his death bed, exonerated Curly Bill, saying he believed it was an accident. Two days after the shooting, he died.

Interestingly, Wyatt's testimony later on behalf of Curly Bill at his court hearing would play a major role in saving the outlaw from the hangman's noose.

In the political election of 1880, Republican Bob Paul was running against Democrat Charlie Shibell for sheriff of Pima County. Paul had a good reputation as a tough lawman while Shibell was more of an administrator. Wyatt remained Shibell's deputy but supported Paul. Shibell won by a few votes but voter fraud was discovered in the San Simon District in the extreme eastern part of the county. The culprits were led by Ike Clanton and Johnny Ringo, who somehow got themselves named election officials. With 50 eligible voters in the district, Shibell received 123 votes and Paul only got one. Wyatt became involved in investigating the fraud and on November 9, 1880 he resigned as Shibell's deputy and Johnny Behan was appointed as his replacement. On April 12, 1881, Bob Paul became Sheriff of Pima County. By that time, Cochise County had already been created.

In the meantime, several of Wyatt's speculative mining and real estate ventures had paid off handsomely.

Political scandalizing in the new boom town and the rowdy acts of the Cowboys brought rise to a Citizens Safety Committee, a group made up mostly of businessmen dedicated to restoring law and order, and improving the tarnished reputation of the town. Throughout the West, vigilance groups such as these were organized when citizens felt the law was not doing enough to thwart crime.

By early 1881, Republicans, led by Mayor John Clum, were in control of Tombstone's city hall. With Democrats controlling the county and Republicans running the city, there were fireworks in the offing. Clum was also editor of the Republican organ, the Tombstone Epitaph.

Not to be denied, the Democrats had their own paper, the Tombstone Nugget, with Harry Woods as publisher and editor. Woods was a member of the 11th Territorial Legislature and had worked to create the new county in the rich Tombstone district.

In the months to come, these two papers would report the events with typical partisan prejudice. Clum's Epitaph would trumpet the law and order, Citizens Safety Committee and its enforcers the Earp brothers, while the Nugget would support Sheriff Behan and the County Ring. And, as the donnybrook between the Cowboys and Earps builds, the Nugget would embrace the Cowboys as playful youngsters out having fun. Both papers attempted to shape opinion on local political matters as well as the feud.

In February, 1881, soon after Cochise County was created, the Democratic Party machine was able to persuade Territorial Governor John C. Fremont to appoint Johnny Behan as Sheriff. Behan was a gregarious, back-slapping political hack who was more interested in padding his pockets than enforcing the law. He was also on friendly terms with the Cowboys and generally took a laissez faire approach to their cattle rustling business.

Wyatt, a political novice, had considered seeking the office of sheriff of Cochise County. Although he was a Republican, he wasn't a serious candidate. The governor's hands were tied anyway. The Democrat-controlled Council or upper chamber of the territorial legislature had the final say on his appointees and Behan was a Democrat and former member of the legislature.

Behan's political cronies John Dunbar became county treasurer and Harry Woods became Behan's undersheriff.

Earlier, Behan had been told that Wyatt planned to seek the office of sheriff so he offered him the position of undersheriff and share in the tax collecting perks. Behan later reneged on his promise. The reason: he owed a political debt to Woods. Politics always came first with Johnny.

The arrival in Tombstone of Sadie Marcus would later serve to deepen the rift between Johnny Behan and Wyatt Earp.

——————————•◦•——————————

Johnny Behan met Sadie Marcus first in October, 1879, when she was touring Arizona with the Gilbert and Sullivan play, H. M. S. Pinafore. She was a slender, young, dark-eyed beauty with a sense for adventure and a lust for excitement. Against her parent's wishes, the headstrong young woman joined an acting troupe doing Gilbert and Sullivan in the boom towns.

Johnny Behan

Behan was quite smitten with Sadie and after becoming sheriff of Cochise County he headed to San Francisco where she was living with her parents. Using all his Irish charm and friendly persuasion he managed to lure her into moving to Tombstone. With the promise of matrimony, she finally agreed.

However, Johnny, a womanizer by habit, was soon up to his old tricks and Sadie became disenchanted and wrote to her father for money to return home. He sent her $300 but smooth-talking Johnny talked her into taking the money, hocking a diamond ring and buying a house, which he put in his own name. She got wise and broke off the relationship in July 1881. When she was down on her luck, it's been claimed that for a time she worked as a courtesan to pay the bills.

Sadie (Josie) Marcus Earp

This photo first appeared in the 1970s.
There is no provenance that it is authentic.

Later that summer, she chanced to meet Wyatt, and the two quickly became friends. He was everything she wanted in a man, except that he was living with Mattie

Blaylock, the woman who had traveled with him all the way from Dodge City. Wyatt Earp met Mattie in Dodge City, or maybe Fort Griffin, Texas sometime in the 1870s. Their relationship began to disintegrate about the time he met Sadie. Wyatt didn't let his "arrangement" with Mattie keep him from seeing Sadie. Sadie Marcus became one of the most unique characters in this frontier drama. She had the distinction of having been intimate with both Behan and Wyatt.

Mattie wound up working as a prostitute in the Arizona mining town of Pinal. She died July 3, 1888, of an overdose of laudanum, after telling friends she was "tired of living." For the most part, Mattie's history is a mystery.

The event leading directly to the West's most famous gunfight occurred on March 15, 1881, when the Benson stage, carrying several thousand dollars in silver bullion was fired upon by four masked men at Drew's Station, about a mile north of Contention City on the San Pedro. Riding shotgun that fateful night was Bob Paul. The driver was Bud Philpot. The stage sped away in a hail of bullets. Another shot entered the back of the stage, fatally wounding a passenger, Peter Roerig.

When word of the robbery reached Tombstone, a posse that included Wyatt, Virgil and Morgan Earp, along with Bat Masterson, Bob Paul, and Sheriff Johnny Behan was formed and went out to pick up the bandit's trail.

They tracked one of the outlaws, Luther King, to a ranch where he was captured without incident. The frightened prisoner identified his accomplices as Bill Leonard, Jim Crane and Harry Head. All were well-known Cowboys.

Most of the posse continued the pursuit of the stage robbers while Johnny Behan escorted the prisoner back to Tombstone. The outlaws had stolen some cattle and driven them along to cover their trail, but the posse kept up relentless pursuit for more than two weeks, covering hundreds of miles and enduring great hardship before giving up the chase. At one point, Behan was supposed to bring fresh horses for the posse but failed to show up with re-mounts. Bob Paul's horse died while Wyatt's and Bat's mounts played out. Paul was able to secure a fresh horse and he, Virgil and Morgan continued the pursuit. Wyatt and Bat wound up having to walk some eighteen miles back to Tombstone.

Luther King didn't remain behind bars long. A large number of Cowboys showed up in town bent on releasing him. Shortly after his arrival at the jail, he walked out the back door and escaped on a horse that had been tied up outside.

Tombstone diarist George Parsons spoke for many when he wrote: "King, the stage robber, escaped early tonight from H. Woods who had been previously notified of an attempt at release to be made. Some of our officials should be hanged. They're a bad lot."

Meanwhile, Virgil's posse, now joined by Behan, Billy Breakenridge, Buckskin Frank Leslie and Ed

Gorman, had endured long periods without food and water. They rode for several more days in pursuit of the outlaws before finally giving up the chase and returning to Tombstone empty-handed.

It was about this same time Wyatt learned that Behan had reneged on his promise to make him undersheriff following the county elections that fall. This, along with his failure to bring fresh mounts to the weary posse, deepened the split between the Earps and the sheriff of Cochise County.

Behan exacerbated the hard feelings when he refused to share the expense money from the county with the other posse members for the pursuit of the outlaws, almost $800, saying he hadn't formally sworn them in as deputies.

Johnny Behan also incurred the wrath of many Tombstone citizens who were fed up with the town's tarnished reputation, claiming he was more interested in collecting taxes than enforcing the law. As county sheriff, he received a ten percent commission on the tax money he collected.

Wyatt's political ambition took a hit when Doc and Big Nose Kate got into a fight. She swore out an affidavit claiming Doc was in on the robbery and the murder of Philpott and Roerig. A warrant was issued and Doc was arrested. Wyatt quickly posted the $5,000 bail. An investigation by the district attorney's office found no evidence that Doc was involved in the robbery and the case was dismissed, but the damage was done. The accusation against Doc Holliday was an embarrassment to Wyatt Earp. The taint of the false charges and the gossip that followed would haunt Wyatt for the rest of his days in Tombstone. He decided the best way to vindicate his friend and get his political campaign back on track was to capture the stage robbers himself. And that set into motion, a chain of events that led directly to the "Gunfight at the OK Corral."

Wyatt decided to enlist the services of Ike Clanton, Frank McLaury and Joe Hill to bring the stage robbers to justice.

Ike Clanton

Wyatt met in secret with the three behind the Oriental Saloon. He offered them the Wells Fargo reward money ($1,200 each) for Leonard, Head and Crane if they would lure the stage robbers to a pre-arranged location where they could be arrested. He would get the glory for their capture and they would split all the reward money. He also promised not to implicate them in any way to the betrayal. Ike wanted to know if Wells Fargo would pay the reward, dead or alive. There was another reason for Ike's willingness to go along with the plot. Bill Leonard had a ranch that Ike coveted. Following the robbery, Ike, thinking Leonard had left the country, moved onto the ranch. When Leonard made it clear he was planning on staying around, Ike figured setting him up for the Earps would not only get him the ranch free and clear, but he'd get the reward money as well.

Wyatt checked with agent Marshall Williams who telegraphed Wells Fargo in San Francisco. They telegraphed back, replying either way, the reward would be paid.

The plan was for Joe Hill to ride over into New Mexico and lure the three stage robbers to a place near the McLaury ranch where the Earps could make the arrest.

The scheme began to unravel when Hill arrived at the New Mexico site in the Animas Valley hideout and learned both Leonard and Head had been killed in a gunfight with Ike and Bill Haslett. The two brothers owned a ranch in the valley that was coveted by the Cowboys. Leonard planned to either run the brothers out of the valley or kill them. Leonard and Head, along with some other Cowboys, stopped at a store, got liquored up and bragged they'd come to kill the Haslett brothers. But someone warned them ahead of time and they decided to choose the time and place for the showdown.

On Friday, June 10, the Haslett brothers came to the store and set up an ambush. When the smoke cleared, Head was dead and Leonard was mortally wounded. Soon after, Jim Crane and fifteen or twenty other friends of Leonard and Head brutally murdered the Haslett brothers in revenge.

The citizens of Cochise County became painfully aware that the Cowboys were now operating as a large gang and would resort to murder if anybody got in their way.

With Head and Leonard out of the way, that left Crane's killing later that summer to finish unraveling Wyatt's plan. In late July, Crane, along with the usual suspects, Johnny Ringo and Curly Bill, were among a group of some twenty-five Cowboys who had been raiding in northern Sonora. They attacked a party of sixteen Mexican smugglers thirty miles south of the border near Fronteras. Four Mexicans were killed and some $4,000 was taken.

About a week later, the Cowboys attacked another Mexican smuggler train, this time on the San Pedro River near Charleston. They got away with about a thousand dollars in gold and silver.

A few days later, thirty Mexican vaqueros rode north across the border into the Animas Valley to recover some stolen livestock. On the way back, they were pursued by about twenty-five Cowboys. A running gunfight ensued and near Guadalupe Pass the Mexicans gave up the fight and the rustlers recovered the herd.

On August 12, Mexican soldiers under the command of Captain Carillo took their revenge. The fifty-man troop tracked the stolen cattle from Sonora into southern New Mexico. Near the border in Guadalupe Canyon they spotted Old Man Clanton and six other men, including Jim Crane, with a herd of cattle. The Mexicans laid in an ambush of their own, killing four and wounding two. Among the dead were Clanton and Crane.

Ike Clanton, Frank McLaury and Joe Hill had lost their blood money. Wyatt also came up empty-handed, losing his chance to capture the stage robbers.

Another stage robbery, this one on the road between Tombstone and Bisbee, occurred on September 8. The stage driver identified the bandits as Pete Spence and one of Johnny Behan's deputies, Frank Stilwell. There was a joke going around the county that Frank Stilwell had held up so many stagecoaches that the stage company's horses were more familiar with his voiced command to "halt" than with the company drivers.

During the holdup, one of the robbers asked the passengers if they had any "sugar." Stilwell always referred to money as "sugar." Also, he'd left some distinctive boot tracks at the scene of the crime. A posse that included Wyatt and Virgil Earp. Marshall Williams, and Fred

Dodge arrested Stilwell and Spence a few days later. Both men posted bail and were released. This story has an ironic twist for the following March 21, Frank Stilwell would be in Tucson to face grand jury charges on the robbery where he would meet face to face with Wyatt Earp one last time.

Naturally, the Cowboys were outraged at being bested again. A few nights later in Tombstone, several Cowboys, including Tom and Frank McLaury, Ike and Billy Clanton, Johnny Ringo and Joe Hill, accosted Morgan Earp, who was alone and unarmed.

Frank McLaury

"I'm telling you Earps something," Frank McLaury said, "You may have arrested Pete Spence and Frank Stilwell, but don't get it in your heads you can arrest me. If you ever lay hands on a McLaury, I'll kill you."

"If the Earps ever have occasion to come after you," Morgan replied, "They'll get you." Then he turned and walked away.

Nothing might have come of the secret deal between Wyatt and Ike except that Wells Fargo agent Marshall Williams had seen Wyatt showing Ike the telegram from the home office in San Francisco offering a reward, dead or alive. He really didn't know anything about the deal but he put two and two together and he walked up to Ike in a saloon one night and chided him for betraying his outlaw cronies. Ike, who'd been drinking heavily went ballistic. Later, he confronted Wyatt and accused him of confiding their deal with the Wells Fargo agent. Wyatt denied the accusation, so Ike claimed he must have told Doc Holliday. Holliday was acquainted with Bill Leonard and Ike feared he would tell the Cowboy about the secret deal. Ike knew he wouldn't live long if Leonard's friends found out about the betrayal. Even though several months passed by without the deal leaking out, he feared the Earps might slip or Holliday might learn of it and tell Leonard.

Again, Wyatt denied telling anybody and sent Morgan to fetch Doc in Tucson. The dentist arrived in Tombstone on Saturday, October 22, and Wyatt asked if he knew anything about the deal to betray the outlaws. Doc said he didn't. Three days later, Doc accosted Ike at the Alhambra Saloon and an argument ensued between the two. After a few minutes, Virgil threatened to arrest both men if they didn't break it up. Doc and Ike separated and went their separate ways but Ike was still in an argumentative mood and accosted Wyatt. Once again, Ike threatened to get the Earps and Doc, saying, "You must not think I won't be after you all in the morning."

Again, Wyatt assured Ike that Doc didn't want to fight but only wanted him to know their secret deal to capture the stage robbers hadn't been revealed.

Later, Ike would give his version saying he was verbally attacked and threatened by Doc, who tried to provoke a fight. Ike claimed he was only trying to avoid trouble.

Ike's situation was getting desperate. If word of his double-cross got out, he was going to be in big trouble with the Cowboys. He'd have to convince them Wyatt had deliberately lied to stir up trouble. It would seem the only way out of this mess would be to force a showdown with the Earps.

Ike made several threats against the Earps, growing more brazen with each shot of whiskey. During these displays of bravado, he always made sure he was unarmed.

By the afternoon of October 25, most of the Cowboys including Ringo and Curly Bill were not in Tombstone. That evening, Ike and Tom McLaury started drinking early at the Grand Hotel, the Cowboy's favorite watering hole. Later they joined an all-night poker game taking place in the Occidental Saloon. The players were an unlikely bunch, considering the events of the past few months. They included Virgil Earp, Johnny Behan, Ike Clanton and Tom McLaury. It appears that none of them let bad blood interfere with a game of cards. It's also likely none realized what the day would bring.

On the morning of that fateful day, Wednesday, October 26, Wyatt was awakened by Ned Boyle, who passed on Ike's latest threats: "As soon as those Damned Earps make their appearance on the street today, the ball will open. We are here to make a fight. We are looking for the sons of bitches."

Later that morning, Ike again threatened to kill the Earps and Holliday on sight. Virgil, sleeping off the all-night poker game, was awakened and told Ike was on the street, armed with a pistol and Winchester, telling passer-bys, "As soon as the Earps show, the ball will open."

Ike then entered Fly's boarding house, where Doc Holliday was sleeping. Mrs. Fly warned Big Nose Kate that Ike was armed and looking for Doc. When awakened, Doc replied, "If God will let me live long enough to get my clothes on, he [Clanton] will see me."

Virgil Earp, well-aware of Ike's threats, walked up behind him and grabbed the rifle barrel. When Ike swung around, Virgil slapped him alongside the ear with his pistol barrel and asked if he was looking for him.

"Yes," Ike replied, "and if I'd seen you a second sooner I would have killed you."

Ike was hauled into court and fined $27.50 for violating gun ordinances. Virgil took Ike's pistol and rifle and deposited them at the Grand Hotel.

A few minutes later, Wyatt met Tom McLaury on the street and challenged him to make a play. When Tom refused, Wyatt decked him with his pistol barrel. Then, Wyatt boldly followed Ike and the McLaury brothers into Spangenberg's gun shop. While they were re-arming, Wyatt noticed Frank's horse was on the boardwalk, another violation of city ordinances. Wyatt grabbed the animal by the bit and backed him into the street. Frank charged out and a heated argument ensued.

Anticipating trouble, Virgil stopped by the Wells Fargo office and picked up a shotgun. Saloonkeeper Bob Hatch approached him and said, "For God sake, hurry down there to the gun shop, for they are all there, and Wyatt is all alone. They are liable to kill him before you get there."

The Cowboys left the gun shop and headed for Dunbar's livery stable. After picking up Billy Clanton's horse, they headed across the street to the OK Corral.

Representatives of the Citizens Safety Committee offered to provide twenty-five armed citizens to help fight the Cowboys but Virgil declined their offer.

Then, Johnny Behan walked up to Virgil and asked what all the excitement was about. Virgil told the sheriff the Cowboys were looking for a fight and requested they go down and disarm them. Behan refused the offer, saying he would go down by himself and disarm them.

Virgil had decided to make the arrest after being informed the Cowboys were on the street and armed. The dye was cast.

Sometime around three o'clock the Earps, (Virgil, Wyatt and Morgan), gathered at Hafford's Saloon, on the corner of Fourth Street and Allen, where they were joined by Doc Holliday. Doc was carrying a cane which he exchanged to Virgil for a sawed-off shotgun. The four men left Hafford's for a rendezvous with destiny. Virgil and Wyatt walked in front, followed by Morgan and Doc. At Fremont, they turned left, heading west towards Third Street.

Sheriff Behan stepped up and said, "Hold up boys, don't go down there or there will be trouble. I have been down there to disarm them."

The group ignored him and walked grimly on. There seems to have been a misunderstanding over Behan's words. Had he disarmed the Cowboys or had he gone down there to disarm them? Believing the sheriff had disarmed the Cowboys, Virgil slid his pistol from the front of his waistband around to the left side. He switched the cane from his left hand to his right. Wyatt put his pistol back in his overcoat pocket.

The Cowboys were standing in the fifteen-foot-wide vacant lot between Fly's Photo Gallery and the Harwood house. They were still packing firearms.

When they were a few feet from the Clantons and

McLaurys, Virgil spoke: "Throw up your hands boys, I want your guns." Billy Clanton and Frank McLaury both had their hands on the butts of their pistols. Tom McLaury was standing next to his horse with his hand on a Winchester still in its scabbard. Virgil heard the sound of hammers being cocked and said, "Hold on, I don't want that!" The time was 2:47 P.M.

Wyatt saw Billy Clanton go for his gun, but knowing Frank McLaury to be the more dangerous, drew his pistol and shot Frank in the stomach. McLaury fell backward, clutching his abdomen. Sure enough, Billy hurried his shot and missed Wyatt. "The fight," as Wyatt later testified, "then became general." Six-guns hammered bullets and flame leaped from the barrels of revolvers. White smoke filled the air as men fell, sprawling in the dirt.

When the shooting began, Tom McLaury's horse started dancing around, preventing him from pulling the rifle from the scabbard. Some versions of the fight have Tom pulling a pistol from inside his shirt and firing two shots. In reality, one of the unknowns of the gunfight is whether or not Tom was packing a pistol. Tom lost his cover when his horse spun away and Doc Holliday cut him down with a double load of buckshot. Tom, gasping for breath, staggered over to the corner of Fremont and Third where he fell, fatally wounded. Doc dropped the shotgun and jerked his pistol and swung it towards Frank McLaury.

With a flurry of motion, Virgil switched the cane to his left hand, pulled his revolver and fired one round at

Frank McLaury and three at Billy Clanton. Ike, claiming he was unarmed, ran up and grabbed Wyatt by the left arm, his bravado suddenly evaporated. Wyatt glared at him, "This fight has commenced," he said, "Go to fighting or get away."

Tom McLaury

Ironically, before Ike turned and ran, he may have inadvertently saved Wyatt's life by accidentally putting himself in the line of fire.

Meanwhile, a bullet hit Morgan. It entered the shoulder on one side and passed through, barely missing the spine. Morgan went down but still had plenty of fight left. He fired and hit Billy in the abdomen. Billy fired again, hitting Virgil in the calf. Virgil was staggered by the gunshot but fired three times hitting Billy twice, in the wrist and the left breast.

Seriously wounded, Frank McLaury staggered into the street, then paused, laid his pistol barrel across his left forearm and aimed at Doc Holliday.

"I've got you now," he said.

"Blaze away! You're a daisy if you have!" Doc replied, firing his pistol, hitting Frank McLaury in the left breast. McLaury fired at the same time, creasing Holliday.

Morgan, on the ground seriously wounded, drew a bead on Frank and dropped him with a shot to the head.

Billy Clanton, game to the end, lay mortally wounded, asking for more bullets. Photographer Camilius S. Fly walked over and picked up his revolver. Billy would live for another hour in agony before expiring from his wounds. Just before dying he said, "Good-bye boys; go away and let me die."

It was all over in less than thirty seconds. More than thirty gunshots were fired.

The Vizina Mine whistle blew, signaling a gathering of the Citizens Safety Committee. A few hours later Ike, who'd been hiding in a local office, was arrested and taken to the county jail. The Tombstone Nugget would report concern over the safety of Ike Clanton. Apparently there was talk of lynching him.

There are more questions than answers. Why had Ike chosen to run instead of to fight that day? It was his big mouth that ignited the fireworks. He talked the talk, but when it came time to walk the walk he ran for his life. He was unarmed and yet he'd been threatening to kill the Earps and Holliday all morning. Ike was always more bark than bite. Much of his baiting of the Earps came when he wasn't packing. He was smart enough to know they wouldn't shoot an unarmed man. Earlier that day Ike had tried unsuccessfully to ambush the Earps and Holliday but Virgil foiled his scheme.

Perhaps he was expecting help from Ringo, Curly Bill and a few other gunmen that day and, when he had enough friends to support his play, he'd have gone to the hotel and gotten his guns. And when they didn't show, he lost his nerve. Were the Cowboys planning to leave town before the fight began? Was Billy trying to get his drunken, hot-headed brother to shut up and go home? The three men didn't appear to be ready for a fight when the Earps arrived on the scene.

As for the Earps and Holliday, certainly Virgil and Wyatt didn't seem to be expecting a gunfight. Virgil had a cane in his gun hand and Wyatt's pistol was in his over-coat pocket. Most likely, they believed Behan had dis-armed the Cowboys.

After the street fight, Sheriff Behan attempted to arrest Wyatt, who glared at him and replied, "I won't be arrested now. You threw us, Johnny."

The dead men were dressed in suits and placed in caskets in the window of Ritter and Evans funeral parlor. Next to the bodies, friends placed a sign that read: "Murdered on the Streets of Tombstone."

Three days after the gunfight, the town council

temporarily suspended Virgil Earp as city marshal, pending investigation of the gunfight. That same day Ike Clanton filed murder charges against the Earps and Doc Holliday.

Initially, newspapers applauded the Earps for taking down some of the lawless element but after Ike and Billy Claiborne claimed the Cowboys were actually trying to surrender, public opinion began to shift. The town became divided: Had the Earps rid the town of outlaws, or had they committed murder? The anti-Earp Tombstone Nugget continued to fan the outrage against the Earps.

Judge Wells Spicer began hearings on the gunfight on November 2. Johnny Behan testified first. On the stand, Behan portrayed himself as a peacemaker who tried unsuccessfully to prevent the gunfight from occurring. He did his best to undermine the Earps. He was either lying through his teeth or was incredibly oblivious to what had been going on for the past several months. His testimony also contained a number of convenient "I don't remember."

Two days later, Will McLaury, an older half-brother of Tom and Frank, and a prominent lawyer from Fort Worth, Texas, arrived and joined the prosecution team. He acquainted himself with members of the Cowboy group who convinced him Tom and Frank were honest ranchers who were murdered by the Earps.

McLaury was able to get Wyatt and Doc charged with murder and locked up without bail. Morgan and Virgil were exempted because of their wounds. Wyatt and Doc spent eighteen days behind bars. Fearing assassination by friends of the slain men, heavily armed members of the vigilance committee maintained a round-the-clock guard around the makeshift jail where Wyatt and Doc were held.

Will McLaury, seeking vengeance for the deaths of his brothers, would stop at nothing to get the Earps and Holliday. It's possible he had a hand in scripting Ike Clanton's testimony in an attempt to twist the events of the past months and paint the Earps as outlaws who killed the McLaury brothers and Billy Clanton because they feared the "honest Cowboys" would expose their nefarious schemes. More likely Ike pulled McLaury into the scheme. Ike was good at twisting the tale. The tactic worked temporarily. The story Ike concocted is believed by many today, including a few historians. Ike tried to portray the Cowboys at the gunfight as harmless and unarmed victims of the brutal Earps. He also accused the Earps of stealing from Wells Fargo, then planning the robberies to cover up their thefts. Ike's well-crafted tale spun a web of intrigue. According to Ike, the Earps were in cahoots with the Benson stage robbers, Crane, Head, Leonard and King. Because they knew too much, the Earps wanted them dead. Ike claimed Wyatt told him he'd "piped off" the money from the stage robbery to Doc Holliday and Bill Leonard.

It's highly unlikely that Wyatt would make such a damaging statement to a known outlaw and cow thief. More important, the stage robbery failed so all money was accounted for.

Ike also claimed the Earps wanted Frank McLaury and Ike out of the way because they also knew too much. Ike seems to have forgotten that Wyatt had an excellent chance to shoot him point blank at the gunfight. On many of the questions, Ike, too, had a convenient case of the "I don't remember."

Ike Clanton not only wanted vengeance for the killing of his brother and the McLaurys, but he also desperately needed a plausible story to allow him back into the good graces of the gang. His self-righteous testimony was laden with errors but has been the source used by several writers who sought to debunk the reputation of the Earp brothers. There were only four stage robberies during the period in question and in each there is overwhelming evidence to prove the Earps could not have been involved. Also, Wells Fargo had undercover operatives working in Tombstone; among them was Fred Dodge. These agents cooperated with the Earps in hunting down the outlaws. It's highly unlikely they would have been working with the Earps had there been the slightest suspicion of unlawful conduct. Tom Fitch, the attorney for the Earps, and Holliday, had a field day shooting holes in Ike's testimony. Ike had presented a tale so contradictory that he actually helped the Earps defense. Fitch would later say, "The witnesses for the prosecution were the best witnesses for the defense."

Judge Spicer concluded the hearings on November 29, and ruled the Earps were justified in their actions. Newspapers from New York to San Francisco had been running daily accounts of the hearing. Much of the nation was now focused on the outlawry in Cochise County.

Ike's uncorroborated testimony, fallacious as it was, did irreparable damage to the Earps reputation in the long run. Most of the debunking of the Earps stems from the twisted tale he told at the hearing.

The Cowboys, under the tutelage of lawyer Will McLaury, lost that round. In their minds, the court of law had failed them. Now they would use the law of the gun to settle matters.

On December 6, President Chester A. Arthur, in a speech to Congress, deplored the lawlessness of Tombstone and proposed enacting legislation that would allow the U.S. Army to act as a posse comitatus. Congress did not act on the proposal so the Army had no authority to intervene.

The outlawry in Cochise County continued. On December 14, the Sandy Bob stage bound for Benson with Mayor John Clum on board was stopped about three miles out of Tombstone. The stage carried no money and remarks were overheard by the bandits indicating they wanted to assassinate the mayor. Clum saved his life by slipping away in the darkness. Threats of assassination included not only the Earps and Holliday, but also Judge Spicer, Mayor Clum and Marshall Williams.

On the evening December 28, Virgil Earp left the Oriental Saloon and headed for the Cosmopolitan Hotel where the Earps had holed up since the threats began. As he reached Fifth Street, the resounding roar of shotgun blasts were heard. Virgil, wounded badly in the left arm and bleeding profusely, walked back to the Oriental to tell Wyatt he'd been shot. Virgil was permanently crippled in the attack. His fighting days in Tombstone were over. After being taken back to his room Virgil said soothingly to his wife Allie, "Never mind, I've got one arm to hug you with."

Immediately after Virgil's wounding, U.S. Marshal C.P. Dake swore Wyatt in as U.S. deputy marshal.

A few weeks later Ike, Fin and Pony Deal faced the court charged with assault with intent to murder. James Bennett, a local citizen testified he found a hat right after the assassination attempt with Ike Clanton's name on it at the building where the assassins had hidden. But Ike's hat wasn't enough to send him to jail and witnesses either wouldn't or couldn't testify they'd seen Ike running from the building. Several witnesses swore Ike was in Charleston when the shooting occurred. All three walked out of the court room free men. Justice worked in strange ways in Cochise County.

Johnny Barnes would later tell Fred Dodge that he did the shooting and Pony Deal was with him.

Where Will McLaury fits into all this is not known but it is possible he helped finance the campaign to avenge the deaths of his brothers and Billy Clanton. Years later he wrote a letter to his father hinting involvement in the retribution.

Wyatt believed Frank Stilwell and Ike were the shooters.

Meanwhile, the outlaws were busy. A few days after the attempted murder of Virgil Earp, on January 6, 1882, the Tombstone-Bisbee stagecoach was robbed again. This time the take was $6,500. One of the bandits took the guard's shotgun and boasted he'd use a Wells Fargo gun to rob the next Wells Fargo strongbox. The next day two men wearing black masks robbed the Tombstone-Benson stage. There was no Wells Fargo strong box on board but the passengers were fleeced for some $1,500. Among the passengers was Wells Fargo's chief special officer, James Hume, who lost two prized pistols in the heist.

Wyatt and Sherman McMaster went to Charleston and, using Cowboy Ben Maynard as a human shield, scoured the town to no avail looking for Ringo, Pony Deal and the Clantons. Ike and Fin surrendered to a posse a few days later, playing for public sympathy by claiming they turned themselves in to seek protection from the Earps. At the hearing, the Clantons and Deal produced alibis and were released for lack of evidence, proving again you couldn't convict a Cowboy in Cochise County.

Judge William Stilwell told Wyatt, "You'll never clean up this crowd this way; next time you'd better leave your prisoners out in the brush where alibis don't count."

Ike Clanton, basking from the successful dismissal of charges for the shooting of Virgil, re-opened the case against the Earps. He persuaded a judge in Contention City to oblige. The Citizens Safety Committee, fearing the Earps would be assassinated, demanded to provide escort and to be present at the trial. The judge sized up the situation and wisely refused to hear the case without any new evidence provided.

In early February, Wyatt sent Ike a note which said in effect, "Let's end this," but Ike refused. He was still convinced the Earps could be convicted for the murder of Billy Clanton and the McLaury brothers. On February 9, he filed murder charges against the Earps and Holliday in the justice of the peace court in Contention. Ike wrote confidently, "I have got the Earps in Jail, and am not going to unhitch."

Believing the trial was a ploy to ambush the Earps and Holliday on the road, twelve well-armed Tombstone citizens accompanied Sheriff Behan on the ride to Contention. Once in the courtroom, Justice of the Peace J. B. Smith remanded the trial back to the county seat at Tombstone. The Earps, through their attorney, argued successfully the charges had already been examined and rejected at the Spicer hearings, where the charges were dismissed. It was ruled that no case could be considered unless new evidence was introduced.

This was a severe setback to Ike, who'd been so confident just a day earlier. Other measures would have to be taken.

On the evening of March 18, tragedy struck again. Wyatt and Morgan were in Hatch's pool hall after attending a show at Scheiffelin Hall. Morgan was shooting pool and Wyatt was sitting in a chair nearby. Suddenly, the upper window of the backdoor was shattered and two shots rang out. Morgan slumped over the table, mortally wounded by a bullet that shattered his spine. Another bullet just missed Wyatt. Witnesses testified before a coroner's jury. The most damaging evidence was given by Marietta Spence, wife of Pete Spence. She claimed her husband, along with Frank Stilwell and Florentino Cruz (aka "Indian Charlie") were the killers. The case came to trial on April 2, but the defense objected to Marietta's testifying and the prosecution dropped the case, apparently because, by law, a woman couldn't testify against her husband.

Morgan Earp

Wyatt didn't believe Pete Spence had anything to do with the assassination of Morgan, believing instead the killers were Frank Stilwell, Johnny Ringo, Curly Bill, Hank Swilling and Indian Charlie. The usual suspects always had friends ready to testify they were miles away from the scene of the crime.

Once again the court system had failed in Cochise County. Wyatt knew the only way justice would be served for the shooting of his brothers would be for him to take the law into his own hands. He would be his brother's avenger, becoming judge, jury and executioner.

Morgan Earp's body was taken to Benson where James would escort it on to Colton, California for burial. Certain that the assassins wouldn't quit until all the Earps were dead, Wyatt convinced Virgil to return to California.

Wyatt and Doc accompanied Virgil and Allie to the train station at Contention where he learned that Frank Stilwell, Ike Clanton and two other Cowboys were watching the trains passing through in hopes of finishing off Virgil.

When the train pulled into the station at Tucson, he and Doc, along with Warren Earp, Turkey Creek Jack Johnson, Texas Jack Vermillion and Sherman McMaster stood guard. Waiting on the platform were Frank Stilwill and Ike Clanton. They quickly disappeared into the crowd when they saw Virgil had an armed escort.

Suddenly, in the darkness outside the train window, Wyatt caught a glimpse of two shotgun barrels shining in the moonlight from behind a flat car. Wyatt was also carrying a shotgun. As he approached the two men, they broke and ran with the marshal in pursuit. He caught up with Stilwell and fired both barrels. He searched unsuccessfully among the moving train cars for Ike, who made another of his patented running exits.

Citizens in Pima and Cochise County followed the turbulent events with interest. George Hand, a Tucson saloonkeeper, recorded in his diary: "Mar. 21. Frank Stillwell {sic} was shot all over, the worst shot-up man that I ever saw. He was found a few hundred yards from the hotel on the railroad tracks. It is supposed to be the work of Doc Holliday and the Earps, but they were not found. Holliday and the Earps knew that Stillwell shot Morgan Earp and they were bound to get him."

Unfortunately, the shooting of Frank Stilwell placed Wyatt outside the law. Unless he, too, could find witnesses to testify that he was miles away at the time of the crime, a practice used with great success by the Cowboys, he was going to stand trial for murder. Wyatt knew if he surrendered to authorities he probably wouldn't live long enough to stand trial. And if, perchance, he did stand trial, he would likely be the scapegoat for all the violence and incur the wrath of justice.

On the evening of March 21, Wyatt and his friends arrived at the Cosmopolitan Hotel in Tombstone. A telegram had arrived from Tucson authorizing Behan to arrest Wyatt for the murder of Frank Stilwell. The telegrapher warned Wyatt, then held the telegram for an hour to give him time to get away. As the Earp party was leaving the hotel, Johnny Behan was waiting to arrest them.

"I want to see you," Behan said.

"Johnny, you may see me once too often," Wyatt replied.

The next to die was Florentino Cruz, (Indian Charlie, as he was known). Cruz had acted as lookout during the assassination of Morgan Earp. He was found at Pete Spence's wood camp in the south pass of the Dragoon Mountains and executed.

Johnny Behan organized a posse made up of Cowboys that included Fin Clanton and Johnny Ringo. Pima County Sheriff Bob Paul refused to join Behan's posse saying, "He persists in cloaking the most notorious outlaws and murderers in Arizona with the authority of the law. I will have nothing to do with such a gang."

Needing cash, Wyatt had borrowed a thousand dollars from a Tombstone mining executive and was supposed to meet the man delivering the money at a water hole called Iron Springs, some thirty miles west of Tombstone, at the southern end of the Whetstone Mountains. On March 23, as they were making a long, uphill ride towards the springs, Wyatt loosened his gun belt to be more comfortable. Suddenly, the stillness resounded with the sound of gunfire as nine Cowboys opened fire. Wyatt and his friends had inadvertently ridden into a hornet's nest of outlaws that included Curly Bill.

Wyatt jumped off his horse, shotgun in hand, prepared to fight. The others, still on horseback, spurred their mounts and scattered helter-skelter for cover, leaving him to fend for himself. Curly Bill and Wyatt, both armed with shotguns, fired at the same time. Curly Bill fired, sending a double load of buckshot that tore a piece off Wyatt's coat. Wyatt raised his scattergun and returned the fire, hitting Curly Bill squarely in the midsection with two loads of buckshot. "His chest was torn open," Wyatt said, "by the big charge of buckshot. He yelled like a demon as he went down."

With Curly Bill out of the fight, Wyatt turned his attention to the other Cowboys, who were ducking and dodging, firing wildly as they ran for cover. Wyatt dropped the empty shotgun and reached for his pistol, but during the excitement, he'd forgotten the loosened gun belt which had slid down around his knees. To make matters worse, his horse, spooked by the gunfire, was doing a war dance. Every time Wyatt would reach down to pull his revolver, the horse would rear, pulling him back up again. The outlaws made their getaway while a pre-occupied Wyatt and his mount were doing a circle dance. One of the Cowboy's bullets ripped through the horn on his saddle and another shot off his boot heel. Wyatt was able get off a few well-aimed shots into a grove of cottonwoods where the Cowboys had sought shelter. One of them, Johnny Barnes, suffered a gunshot wound.

Four days later, the Earp party rode into Colonel Henry Clay Hooker's Sierra Bonita ranch at the north end of the Sulphur Springs Valley. Wyatt and his men were treated with the generous hospitality for which the ranch was noted. Later that evening they rode on.

The next day Johnny Behan's posse arrived at the Hooker ranch, demanding food and the whereabouts of Wyatt Earp. The rancher told the sheriff he didn't know where Wyatt was and wouldn't tell if he knew.

Behan accused Hooker of "upholding murderers and outlaws."

Hooker responded "I know the Earps and I know you and I know they have always treated me like a gentleman. Damn such laws and damn you, and damn your posse. They are a set of horse thieves and outlaws."

At this point, one of the posse members jumped into the fracas saying, "Damn the son of a bitch. He knows where they are. Let's make him tell."

About that time, one of Hooker's men drew down on the posse with his Winchester. "You can't come here into a gentleman's yard and call him a 'son of a bitch.' Now you skin it back! Skin it back!"

Behan, never one to fight if there was a way out, backed down.

Hooker was too much of a gentleman to send the posse away on empty stomachs. They were invited to dinner but Behan's outlaw friends were made to eat at separate tables.

Later that evening, Behan approached the cow-puncher who'd covered Colonel Hooker and offered him a hundred dollar diamond stud from his shirt if he'd not say anything about the incident. Behan's bribe didn't work. The story later appeared in the Epitaph.

Behan then tried to secure scouts from nearby Fort Grant but the commanding officer, aware of Hooker's response, refused.

By now, most of the Cowboys involved in the shootings of the Virgil and Morgan Earp were either dead or had left the country. Wyatt and his men rode for Silver City, New Mexico, arriving there on April 8. During the next few weeks the Nugget printed stories of gunfights, each with an eyewitness account of the killing of Wyatt Earp. Like Mark Twain's death, the reports were greatly exaggerated. Wyatt was next heard from in Gunnison, Colorado, while Doc went on to Denver.

In June, authorities in Arizona attempted to have Wyatt and Doc extradited from Colorado to stand trial for the murder of Frank Stilwell. But Governor F. W. Pitkin, fearing the men wouldn't live long enough to stand trial, refused extradition.

On July 14, the body of Johnny Ringo was found at the foot of a large oak tree at Turkey Creek, in the foothills of the western slope of the Chiricahua Mountains. He'd been dead about twenty-four hours and had already begun to turn black. Ringo died with his boots off. His undershirt was torn in half and wrapped around his feet. He was found beneath a blackjack oak on the edge of the creek, with a bullet in his head. A pistol with one bullet missing was clenched in his right hand. Two cartridge belts were wrapped around his waist; one was buckled upside down. A piece of his hair was missing, as if he'd been scalped. A coroner's jury ruled it suicide. Years later, Billy Breakenridge blamed Buckskin Frank Leslie. Others claimed Mike O'Rourke (better known as "Johnny-Behind-the-Duece") killed Ringo, and was, in turn, gunned down by Ringo's pal, Pony Diehl (Deal), who was, in turn, iced by somebody else. Most experts, however, believe Ringo committed suicide.

Johnny Ringo

On November 14, the last of Tombstone's famous gun duels occurred when Buckskin Frank Leslie gunned down Billy Claiborne in front of the Oriental Saloon. It was later claimed Claiborne made some taunting remarks about Leslie killing Ringo.

Will McLaury's vendetta against the Earps had been costly. He later wrote the experience was "very unfortunate—as to my health—and badly injured me as to money matters—and none of the results have been satisfactory—the only result is the Death of Morgan and crippling of Virgil Earp and the death of McMasters." He was wrong on the last point. Wyatt said Sherman McMaster was not killed until 1898 in the Spanish American War.

Ike and Fin Clanton moved their rustling operation north into the White Mountains where Ike was killed on June 1, 1887, by a correspondence school detective named J. V. Brighton. Not surprisingly, Ike was shot while running away. One thing that can be said about Ike; he was consistent. Fin was charged with grand larceny and was sentenced to ten years in the Yuma Territorial Prison but was pardoned after serving only two years. He moved to Globe where he died in a wagon accident in 1906.

Doc Holliday died of tuberculosis on November 8, 1887, in a hotel room in Glenwood Springs, Colorado. Lying in bed that final day, he asked for a shot of whiskey, then looked down at his bare feet and muttered characteristically, "This is funny!"

Johnny Behan was pretty much disgraced by the events that took place in Cochise County during his tenure as sheriff, and lost his party's nomination to Larkin Carr. Behan's association with the outlaw element was too much for the Democratic Party hierarchy and he fell out of favor.

While sheriff, Behan was quite adept at padding his expenses and collecting taxes. Records show he was earning some $25,000 a year as sheriff when the annual salary was only $2,500. He was indicted by a grand jury for continuing to collect taxes after he left office.

Johnny continued to live off the public trough, eventually becoming a politically appointed superintendent at the Territorial Prison at Yuma, serving from 1887 to 1890. He enlisted in the army during the Spanish-American War and later served in China during the Boxer Rebellion. He died in Tucson in 1912.

Warren Earp, the youngest of the fighting brothers, was shot and killed in a barroom fight in Willcox on July 6, 1900, by a cowboy named Johnny Boyette. Earp was unarmed but the jury ruled self-defense.

Mary Catherine Harony, aka Big Nose Kate Elder Fisher, died in the Arizona Pioneers Home at Prescott in 1940. Photographs reveal a normal sized nose so it's been speculated she might have earned her nickname from sticking her nose into everybody's business. Some might wonder how a woman like Kate wound up in the respectable Pioneers Home. Prescott historian Budge Ruffner suggested that some Arizonans, "gave their lives for honor but she gave her honor for life."

Wyatt and Virgil continued their restless wandering. For a time Virgil and Allie lived in Colton, California, where he served as town marshal, before moving to

Vanderbilt, near the Arizona-Nevada border. A year later, they moved to Cripple Creek, Colorado, where he and Wyatt opened a saloon. In 1895, he and Allie moved back to Prescott where he invested in a mine and worked as a deputy sheriff. San Diego was their next stop where he and Wyatt were again involved in some business ventures.

Virgil was the only one of the fighting Earp brothers to have a child but he was unaware of it for many years. While still a teenager, he'd married a girl named Ellen Rysdam. Then, he'd gone off to fight in the Civil War. Somehow she believed he'd died in battle so she moved west to Oregon with her family. There, she gave birth to Virgil's child, a girl, Nellie Jane. Virgil believed Ellen had died while he was away. Many years later, the daughter, now grown, heard about the famous Virgil Earp and contacted him. In 1899, Virgil and Allie went to Portland where he was re-united with his ex-wife and daughter. It must have been a poignant, but joyful occasion for Virgil as he and Allie had had no children.

The new boom town of Goldfield, Nevada was the next residence for Virgil and Allie.

Virgil was still working as a lawman in Goldfield, Nevada, in 1905, when he died of pneumonia. His daughter had his body buried at her hometown of Portland, Oregon. Two weeks after Virgil's death, the family patriarch, Nicholas Porter Earp, passed away in California. Allie Earp died in 1947.

In December 1882, Wyatt met up with Sadie, who had gone home to San Francisco and they headed for Gunnison, Colorado. The next year he led a group of "desperate men" to help his old friend Luke Short, in what became known as the "Dodge City War." The presence of several well-known gunfighters was enough to cause the other side to back down without a fight. A year later, he and Sadie headed for Eagle, Idaho, for a time, then it was off to Cripple Creek, Colorado.

During the late 1890s, Wyatt involved himself in several entrepreneurial ventures including race horses, real estate and gambling. While in San Francisco, in December 1896, he agreed to referee the heavyweight championship fight between Cornishman Bob Fitzsimmons and "Sailor" Tom Sharkey. It would be something that he would greatly regret.

It's been called the greatest sporting event west of the Mississippi in the 19 century. Before the fight began, an incident occurred that would become an embarrassment for Wyatt in the days to come. Just before the fight began, a police captain noticed a bulge in Wyatt's pocket. The lawman asked if he was carrying a gun. Wyatt answered that he was and gave his weapon to the officer. He was so used to carrying a gun that he'd completely forgotten to leave it at home.

The fight began and the favorite, Fitzsimmons, was in control even though it appeared that Sharkey fouled him several times. Sharkey was saved by the bell twice before the eighth round. In the eighth round, Fitzsimmons caught Sharkey with a punch to the stomach. Sharkey went down, clutching his groin. The Cornishman seemed amused by the antics of the sailor, but Wyatt walked over to Sharkey's corner and declared him the winner on a foul. The winner of the fight had to be carried from the ring. Afterwards, when the official medical examiner for the National Athletic Club and four other physicians tried to see Sharkey to examine the extent of his injury, they were refused admission to his dressing room.

The decision caused quite a furor. Wyatt was accused of throwing the fight for Sharkey. Wyatt denied favoring, saying that if he had been so inclined to favor anybody it would have been Fitzsimmons, who had been introduced to him by his best friend, Bat Masterson. He went on to say that he called it the way he saw it. The public outcry was great and there were charges the fight had been fixed.

To add insult to injury, he was also fined fifty dollars for carrying a concealed weapon.

It was never determined exactly what happened at the fight. There are three possibilities: Fitzsimmons fouled Sharkey and Wyatt made the right call; Sharkey's acting duped Wyatt into believing he was fouled; there was a fix and Wyatt was a part of it. Knowing Wyatt's character, it's highly unlikely he was part of a fix. Sharkey's supporters certainly believed he was fouled and had Wyatt not called a foul and awarded the fight to their man they would have raised as much a ruckus as Fitzsimmons' fans did. Wyatt had refereed many bare-knuckle fights in his time but this was his first under boxing's new Rules of

Queensbury. In short, he was not qualified to referee a bout of such importance and should have never stepped into the ring.

Newspapers had a field day castigating Wyatt. It was the second time in his career that he'd been a victim of vicious attacks by the press. Through it all, Wyatt was steadfast in defending his decision as just and fair.

The following summer Wyatt and Sadie left for the goldfields of Alaska. Gold had been discovered in the Klondike and they joined the rush of adventurers in search of pay dirt, opening a saloon in Nome. After two years in the "Land of the Midnight Sun" Wyatt pulled up stakes and cashed in, taking home some $85,000 in profits. In early 1902, they were back in business in the boom town of Tonopah, Nevada.

It was about this time Theodore Roosevelt was entertaining some of the old gunfighters when the president's press secretary, Stuart Lake, overheard Bat Masterson say something to the effect that the story of the true West would never be known until Wyatt Earp decided to tell his story. After Bat Masterson died in 1921, Lake decided it was time to go west and talk to Wyatt. The result was Wyatt Earp: Frontier Marshal.

The book portrayed Earp as the epitome of the western lawman and elevated him to superstar status. It was the inspiration for hundreds of books, booklets, movie and television scripts. Wyatt had died by the time the book was published and it's difficult to say what he would have had to say about it. Stuart Lake was a gifted writer with a way with words and it's difficult to separate what were Wyatt's words and the words from Lake's fertile imagination.

Although the Gunfight at OK Corral might have been the defining moment of Wyatt Earp's life, it says little about the man. He spent a little more than two years in Tombstone and lived another 47 years after he left the "Town Too Tough To Die." His detractors have made much of his savage vendetta following the wounding of Virgil and murder of Morgan, saying he operated outside the law. He told biographer Stuart Lake just before his death if he'd been willing to go outside the law earlier Morgan would still be alive. "It's a pretty high price to ask a man to pay for trying to shoot square," he said.

Wyatt's entire life was one of continuous adventure. He was a product of his times, living life to the hilt. He had an unquenchable thirst for gambling—high stakes, low stakes—anything as long as it was a game of chance. That's how he lived his life.

Wyatt Earp died peacefully in his sleep at 8:05 on the morning of January 13, 1929.

Sadie had remained faithfully by his side for nearly 50 years. Since they had no children and most of his family was gone, she took his ashes home to San Francisco. She died in 1944 and rests beside him in a Jewish cemetery in Colma, a few miles south of San Francisco.

The author would like to thank noted Wyatt Earp author, Casey Tefertiller for his editing of this work.

For Further Reading:

Barra, Allen. *Inventing Wyatt Earp: His Life and Many Legends*. New York. Carroll and Graf, 1998.

Bell, Bob Boze. *The Illustrated Life and Times of Billy the Kid*. Cave Creek: Boze Books, 1992.

_____. *The Illustrated Life and Times of Doc Holliday*. Phoenix: Tri Star Boze, 1994.

_____. *The Illustrated Life and Times of Wyatt Earp*. Phoenix: Tri Star Boze, 1994.

_____. *Outlaws and Gunfighters of the Wild West*. Phoenix: Tri Star Boze, 1999.

_____. *Classic Gunfights: Volume One*. Phoenix: Tri Star Boze, 2003.

Erwin, Richard E. *The Truth About Wyatt Earp*. Carpinteria, CA.: The OK Press, 1993.

Fattig, Timothy. *Wyatt Earp: The Biography*. Honolulu, Hawaii, Talei Publishers, 2002.

Gatto, Steve. *Johnny Ringo*. Lansing, Michigan: Protar House, 2002.

_____. *Curly Bill*. Lansing, Michigan: Protar House, 2003.

Marks, Paula Mitchell. *And Die In The West*. New York, NY.: William Morrow and Co., 1989.

Parsons, George W. *The Private Journal of George W. Parsons Tombstone Epitaph*. Tombstone AZ., 1972.

Roberts, Dr. Gary. *Doc Holliday: The Life and the Legend*. Hoboken, New Jersey: John Wiley and Sons, Inc., 2006.

Tanner, Karen Holliday. *Doc Holliday: A Family Portrait*. Norman: University of Oklahoma Press, 1998.

Tefertiller, Casey. *Wyatt Earp: The Life Behind the Legend*. New York: John Wiley and Sons Inc., 1997.

Trimble, Marshall. *Arizona Adventure*. Rev. ed. Phoenix: Golden West Publishers, 2003.

To Learn More About How The Myth Was Made:

Lake, Stuart. *Wyatt Earp: Frontier Marshal*. Boston, MA: Houghton Mifflin Co., 1931.

Burns, Walter Noble. *Tombstone: An Iliad of the Southwest*. New York: Doubleday and Co., 1928.

Myers, John Myers. *The Last Chance: Tombstone's Early Years*. New York: E. P. Dutton., 1950.

To learn more about what the other side had to say:

Walters, Frank. *The Earp Brothers of Tombstone*. New York: Clarkson N. Potter, 1960.

Bartholomew, Ed. *Wyatt Earp: The Man and the Myth*. Toyahvale, TX: Frontier Book Co., 1963.

_____ Wyatt Earp: *The Untold Story*. Toyahvale, TX: Frontier Book Co., 1964.

Other sources for general references:

Nash, Jay Robert. *Encyclopedia of Lawmen and Outlaws.* New York: Paragon House, 1992.

Metz, Leon. *The Encyclopedia of Lawmen, Outlaws, and Gunfighters.* New York, NY: Facts on File Inc., 2003.

O'Neal, Bill. *Encyclopedia of Western Gunfighters.* Norman: University of Oklahoma Press, 1979.

Rosa, Joe. *The Gunfighter: Man or Myth?* Norman: University of Oklahoma Press, 1969.

Index

More Books by American Traveler Press

From Marshall Trimble

Arizona Adventure!
5½ x 8½—160 Pages . . . $9.95

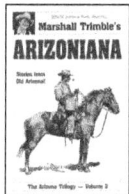

In Old Arizona
5½ x 8½—160 Pages . . . $9.95

Arizoniana
5½ x 8½—160 Pages . . . $9.95

Wild West Heroes and Rogues:
Wyatt Earp
5½ x 8½—80 Pages . . . $6.95

From Charles Lauer

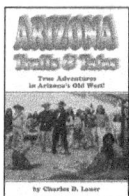

Arizona Trails & Tales
5½ x 8½—192 Pages . . . $14.95

Tales of Arizona Territory
5½ x 8½—160 Pages . . . $14.95

Arrows, Bullets and Saddle Sores
5½ x 8½—184 pages. . . $9.95

Old West Adventures
5½ x 8½—176 pages. . . $9.95

Other Titles

Arizona Legends and Lore
5½ x 8½—176 Pages . . . $9.95

Cowboy Slang
5½ x 8½—128 Pages . . . $9.95

Ghost Towns and
Historical Haunts in Arizona
5 ½ x 8 ½—144 pages . . . $9.95

ORDER BLANK

AMERICAN TRAVELER PRESS

☼ **5738 North Central Avenue • Phoenix, AZ 85012**

www.americantravelerpress.com • 1-800-521-9221 • FAX 602-234-3062

Qty	Title	Price	Amount
	Arizona Adventure	9.95	
	Arizona Cookbook	9.95	
	Arizona Legends and Lore	9.95	
	Arizona Territory Cookbook	9.95	
	Arizona Trails and Tales	14.95	
	Arizoniana	9.95	
	Arrows, Bullets and Saddle Sores	9.95	
	Billy the Kid Cookbook	9.95	
	Cowboy Slang	9.95	
	Days of the West	14.95	
	Desert Survival Handbook	8.95	
	Discover Arizona!	6.95	
	Experience Jerome	6.95	
	Finding Gold in the Desert	5.95	
	Ghost Towns and Historical Haunts in Arizona	12.95	
	Haunted Arizona	12.95	
	Hiking Arizona	6.95	
	In Old Arizona	9.95	
	Mavericks—Ten Uncorralled Westerners	5.00	
	Old West Adventures in Arizona	9.95	
	Prehistoric Arizona	5.00	
	Tales of Arizona Territory	14.95	
	Wild West Heroes & Rogues: Wyatt Earp	6.95	

| **U.S. Shipping & Handling Add:**
(Shipping to all other countries see website.) | 1-3 Books $3.00
4+ Books $5.00 | |
| Arizona residents add 9.3% sales tax | | |

Total $_____
(Payable in U.S. funds)

☐ My Check or Money Order Enclosed

☐ MasterCard ☐ VISA ☐ AMEX ☐ Discover   Verification code_____

Acct. No. _____ Exp. Date _____

Signature _____

Name _____ Phone _____

Address _____

City/State/Zip _____

Call for a FREE catalog of all our titles — Prices subject to change —

www.ingramcontent.com/pod-product-compliance
Lightning Source LLC
Chambersburg PA
CBHW071835020426
42331CB00007B/1740